Jack Prelutsky
IT'S HALLOWEEN
pictures by Marylin Hafner

ISBN 0-590-41536-0

12 11 10 9 8 7 6

1 2/9

Printed in the U.S.A.

28

SCHOLASTIC INC.
New York Toronto London Auckland Sydney

With love to Diane W.
May monsters never trouble you · J.P.

For Abigail, Jennifer, and Amanda —
my original trick-or-treaters · M.H.

CONTENTS

MY
GLASS
IS
RUN
HERE
LIES THE

IT'S HALLOWEEN

It's Halloween! It's Halloween!
The moon is full and bright
And we shall see what can't be seen
On any other night:

Skeletons and ghosts and ghouls,
Grinning goblins fighting duels,
Werewolves rising from their tombs,
Witches on their magic brooms.

In masks and gowns
we haunt the street
And knock on doors
for trick or treat.

Tonight we are
the king and queen,
For oh tonight
it's Halloween!

SKELETON PARADE

The skeletons are out tonight,
They march about the street
With bony bodies, bony heads
And bony hands and feet.

Bony bony bony bones
with nothing in between,
Up and down and all around
They march on Halloween.

THE TRICKSTERS

Three Halloween tricksters are we—
My sister, my brother and me.

We roam through the streets

Playing tricks, getting treats—

Three Halloween tricksters are we.

Sister's a witch dressed in black,

Brother wears bones front and back,

I'm a ghost with no face

In an old pillowcase—

Three Halloween tricksters are we.

We are scary as scary can be—

My sister, my brother and me.

We frighten each other,

We even scare mother—

Three Halloween tricksters are we.

PUMPKIN

We bought a fat

orange pumpkin,

The plumpest sort

they sell.

We neatly scooped

the inside out

And only left

the shell.

We carved a funny
funny-face
Of silly shape
and size,
A pointy nose,
a jagged mouth
And two enormous eyes.

over just
a little...

We set it in a window
And we put
    a candle in,
Then lit it up
    for all to see
Our jack-o'-lantern grin.

COUNTDOWN

There are ten ghosts
in the pantry,

There are nine
upon the stairs,

There are eight ghosts
in the attic,

There are seven
on the chairs,

There are six
within the kitchen,

There are five
along the hall,

There are four
upon the ceiling,

There are three
upon the wall,

There are two ghosts

on the carpet,

Doing things

that ghosts will do,

There is one ghost

right

behind me

Who is oh so quiet . . .

THE GOBLIN

There's a goblin as green
As a goblin can be
Who is sitting outside
And is waiting for me.
When he knocked on my door
And said softly, "Come play!"
I answered, "No thank you,
Now please, go away!"

But the goblin as green

As a goblin can be

Is still sitting outside

And is waiting for me.

Give us candy,
give us cake,
give us something
sweet to take.

You had better do it quick or we'll surely play a trick.
Trick or treat, trick or treat, give us something good to eat.

BOBBING FOR APPLES

Watch us bobbing for an apple,

For an apple apple apple,

But no apple apple apple,

Not an apple can I get.

Oh I cannot catch an apple,

Not one apple apple apple.

Though my sister got an apple,

All I got was soaking wet.

HAUNTED HOUSE

There's a house
  upon the hilltop
We will not go inside
For that is where
  the witches live,
Where ghosts
  and goblins hide.

Tonight they have
their party,
All the lights are
burning bright,

But oh we will not

   go inside

The haunted house tonight.

The demons there are whirling
And the spirits swirl about.
They sing their songs to Halloween.
"Come join the fun," they shout.

But we do not want to go there

So we run with all our might

And oh we will not go inside

The haunted house tonight.

BLACK CAT

A cat as black

As blackest coal

Is out upon

His midnight stroll.

His steps are soft,

His walk is slow,

His eyes are gold,

They flash and glow.

And so I run

And so I duck,

I do not need

His black-cat luck.

GHOST

I saw a ghost
 that stared and stared
And I stood still
 and acted scared.
But that was just
 a big pretend.

I knew that ghost . . .

. . . it was my friend!

HAPPY HALLOWEEN

It's late and we are sleepy,
The air is cold and still.
Our jack-o'-lantern grins at us
Upon the window sill.

We're stuffed with cake and candy

And we've had a lot of fun,

But now it's time to go to bed

And dream of all we've done.

We'll dream of ghosts and goblins
And of witches that we've seen,

And we'll dream of trick-or-treating
On this happy Halloween.